Pink Elep

A Journey into En

By Mark Laty, MD.

About The Book

This guide is the culmination of twenty years of experience in the treatment of psychiatric and addictive conditions and the never-ending search for the ultimate truth.

Although this book is based on scientific research and medical facts, it is also spiritual, philosophical, and psychological. This guide is infused with wisdom taken from countless ancient literatures and records such as the work of Confucius, Thoth, Taoism, Shinto, Aristotle, Plato, and Zen Buddhism. It is a true journey into the mind and the soul.

After twenty years of working with both celebrities and 'regular' people in the United States and around the world struggling with mental conditions and addictions, I came up with a system that can help everyone. Even if you don't have a psychiatric problem or addiction, this system can still benefit you, as this guide is simply a manual of knowledge and enlightenment.

Introduction

"What lies in our power to do, it lies in our power not to do." ***—Aristotle (384–322 BC)***

Not long ago, just after a famous celebrity passed away due to an overdose, I had an interview with a young TV reporter who asked me for my take on addiction.

I said, "Addiction is like a neurological hijack of the brain, someone else is in control." And I paused.

There was a moment of uncomfortable silence while she waited for me to say more, but in reality, there was not much to add; that simple statement summarized it all. But then again, aren't we all tormented souls? Aren't we all victims of circumstances?

Imagine waking up one day to find yourself lost and alone in the middle of a vast, endless desert, surrounded by nothing but dunes of sand as far as your eyes can see, and you realize that if no one shows up soon to rescue you, you're going to die. After a couple of days, when you're all dried up, burned by the scorching sun, and you've lost all hope, you see two Bedouins on camels approaching from a distance and going in opposite directions. One is coming from the north, and the other is coming from the south, and when they come closer, you realize that one of them is a demon, and the other one is an angel. They cross paths at exactly where you stand, but then they keep moving, as if you are invisible.

The angel carries water, and the demon carries your drug of choice. You have to make a critical decision in a split second; you have to choose which of the camel men to follow. But first, you need to scream for help. You need to shout, "Help! Help! Help!" so they can hear you.

Fortunately, you were able to, and so both camel men stop and wait for you to decide which one of them should help you. But for you, it is a no-brainer. You choose the obvious. You follow the demon, because he's got your fix. The demon looks at you with his glowing, devilish eyes and smiles. He gives you your drug of choice, and you immediately consume it right on the spot, and then you stare at the sun and ride your pink elephant as you fade out into darkness.

You see, addiction is not a disease like most of the so called "scholars" claim. In my opinion, addiction is an "obsession," a state of mind. It is a decision of "no-decision." It is physical more than psychological and actual more than spiritual. It is a "self-fulfilled prophecy," so to speak.

I would say everyone on this planet is addicted to something. Even animals and insects have addiction problem. Should I tell you the story of the addicted ants in my house?

I used to smoke and drink, and perhaps it goes without saying that my house was mess. To make the long story short, I used to roll tobacco and smoke it and drink a glass of wine every night after work while watching TV, and since I was single and messy, I didn't clean after myself. I left everything on the coffee table.

After a while, I noticed an army of ants—let's call them group A—crawling on the glass of wine that I left the night before, so I would clean the coffee table where I left the glass of wine, and I didn't think much of it. Then I noticed a different group of ants—let's call them group B—that looked different than the wine ants. The Group B ants were a little bigger, and they dragged tobacco pieces from the other end of the table where I used to leave the tobacco pouch. Again, in the beginning I didn't think much of it. But after a while, I discovered that Group A continued to crawl to the spot where I left the glass of wine, and Group B continued to surround and consume the tobacco.

This observation continued for years, and no matter what I did, those ants didn't leave me alone. They would just show up to have tobacco and wine. So obviously what we have here are two groups of ants, one addicted to tobacco, and the other addicted to alcohol. I'm sure you've heard of smoking apes, alcoholic monkeys, and cocaine rats. The brain is a highly addicted organ, even in the animal kingdom.

You see, people continue their addiction to the point of destruction not because they want to, but because they are trapped inside a circle of confusion, trapped inside an iron ball with no windows and no exits. Deep inside that iron sphere, they feel that they've reached a point of no return and that this is their destiny; this is their best comfort zone. This is where they meet their gods and their demons. They feel helpless and do not know where, how, or even why to start running. They wonder what the point is. They are victims of circumstances. Not to mention, of course, that they are already designed biologically to become addicts, so the circle of confusion becomes even tighter and more powerful.

People continue their addiction and embrace it because they are simply at the end of their rope, being pulled by unknown forces and seduced by pink elephants. They've given up. Because when you think about it, why would anyone want to destroy his or her life? After all, people get drugs because they want to get high, to feel good, to be happy. On the other hand, people continue to use drugs because they want to numb their pain; they are running away from something. They are afraid of something; fear is the ultimate enemy. Fear is where the problem lies. Fear is what really fucks you up.

Everyone has some kind of addiction; some of us are addicted to drugs, some to alcohol, and many to nicotine. Some of us are addicted to food, sex, gambling, drama, masturbation, lies, fame, money, rock and roll, or even killing—yes, that's right, murder, such as serial killers—and the list goes on and on.

Neurobiologically, addiction to alcohol and or drugs is not much different from addiction to food, for example, in the sense that it also triggers certain chemicals in the brain such as dopamine, serotonin, adrenaline and/or enkephalin (or endorphins), which are endogenous opioid peptides that are involved in the mechanism of addiction. Basically, either way you're screwed. However, I must add that certain drugs or conditions might not alter your state of mind to a great degree, such as nicotine, sex, or chocolate, for example. Therefore, you might be able to function in life even if you are addicted to sex or cigarettes, but you can't function properly if you are addicted to opiates, cocaine, Xanax or alcohol. So the degree of dysfunction may vary from one addiction to another.

Mind-altering drugs such as alcohol, opiates, stimulants, inhalants, LSD, PCP, MDMA (molly), and so forth are severely disabling drugs. I know most people might say, "Marijuana is good for you. It is natural." Well, so is water hemlock and Ricin. They are natural too, but they are the deadliest poisons.

Don't get me wrong, I'm not against pot. It's not as bad as other drugs, and it is not very addictive, but I always say, "Cigarettes destroy your health, but marijuana destroys your future." Before you start smoking pot, make sure you have a future. Because once you start on that path, you become lazy, and your concentration goes down the drain. One thing leads to another, and you find yourself smoking all kinds of shit. Your choice.

Some might say addiction to food or gambling is not really an addiction—it is just a fancy way of saying, "They just can't stop eating," or of observing a person with some seriously bad habits. However, the bottom line is not really about the definition of addiction or analyzing the condition as much as understanding it and treating it, or at least finding a solution.

If the substance—or the condition, I should say—is causing dysfunction, damage, or destruction in any aspect of your life, such as your work, your health, your sex life, your relationships with others, or even if it affects your psychological state of mind, then you have a serious problem. You're an addict and you need to get help if: you walk around feeling guilty about your habit or constantly thinking that you need to stop it or cut down on it; you can't wait to get your next fix because it is constantly on your mind; or you get annoyed when someone calls you out on it. The problem is, you might just not know that you're an addict.

Here are 3 Steps of knowledge and enlightenment that will allow you to identify, acknowledge, and overcome your addictive behaviors.

Chapter One

Honesty

"I want you to be everything that's you, deep at the center of your being." —Confucius (551–479 BC)

The minute you admit to yourself that you have a problem, you've already started your journey towards enlightenment. Honesty is your first step toward freedom. Everything else after that is just a matter of time. But I warn you, my brothers and sisters: before you take this first step, sit back and meditate. Sit back and make a decision, because without a decision, there is no journey and no point reading this book.

When Michael entered my office at the rehabilitation facility, I asked, "Why are you here, Michael?"

His answer was, "Honestly, Doc, I have no idea why I'm here. My wife wanted me to come here. She said, 'If you don't go to rehab, I'm gonna divorce you.' You know what they say, 'happy wife happy life.' That's why I'm here." And he started laughing.

I replied, "So you don't think you have a problem with alcohol?"

Michael didn't even bother saying yes or no, he just shook his head as if to say, *why am I even here?*

I asked, "Do you think you're an alcoholic?"

"I don't think so."

"Do you think you drink too much?"

Michael sighed and leaned back so that his chair was only resting on the back two legs. "Just like anyone else. On weekends, on occasions, that's all."

"Do you have any DUI's?"

"Well…" Michael hesitated. "I do have three DUI's, but I wasn't drunk. I was just fine. Believe me, Doc, the police in this country are a bunch of assholes. I mean, I don't have to tell you. He stopped me the first time not because I was drunk, but because I was screaming out of the window at some chick with big tits. I was horny, man, I was single back then and so he stopped me because I was too loud, that's all."

"What about the second time?"

Michael shrugged and brought the front legs of his chair back down with a thud. "The second time, I was going too fast, not drunk though. And the third time, some Asian lady hit my car from the back, and it wasn't even my fault, and when the police came—because that dumb bitch called the police—he smelled alcohol on me."

"What about work?" I asked.

He glared at me. "What about it?"

"Do you have a problem at your work?"

"Well... I don't work. I'm unemployed at the moment. Why are you asking me all these questions, man?"

"Why are you unemployed?"

"OK fine. Listen, I can't find a job. I'm white, and white people can't find jobs anymore. Look around you, Doc, there is not even one homeless black person in the entire country. All the homeless folks now are white; don't tell me you haven't noticed that?"

"What was your job before?" I asked, redirecting the conversation.

"I was a manager at a retail company. I got fired and they hired a black woman to replace me. Doc, OK I might have a little problem with drinking, but I make sense."

"Then what happened?"

"I don't know. I didn't like my boss. He was an asshole, and he was too judgmental. I was late two times in five years, and he started being a wiseass with me so I told him to fuck off. You know, Doc, I'm not bragging about it, but I'm a UFC fighter, I could've rearranged his ugly motherfucker face in one round kick." His face turned red, his eyes glazing over and his fists clenching in his lap like he was imagining his ex-boss standing before him. "In fact," he continued, "I should've; I would've made a lot of people happy at work. Truthfully, Doc, I still regret it. I'm a coward, because if had any balls, I would've killed that motherfucker."

I paused, waiting for his fists to unfurl. "How long have you been without a job now, Michael?" I asked.

"Two years. I did work at a few places but I didn't like them. Come on, Doc, what is this some kind of interrogation?" Michael scooted up in his seat, clutching his arm rests. "White people are getting fired and replaced by blacks because of this affirmative action shit. That is what I call racism, Doc, not the one you hear all the time on the news. A Hispanic man or a woman works ten times as hard as a black one, yet they hire the black; what do you call that? We even had a black president, and they're still shouting and screaming racism. It's a game, Doc, it's a game. The system is stupid and broken, but you can't admit it, because you don't want to lose your job.

"What does your wife think, Michael?" I said, navigating the conversation back to him.

Michael waved his hand through the air like he was shoeing a fly. "You don't understand, Doc, my wife is an old-fashioned woman, and I think she's the one who needs psychiatric help, not me. She's obsessive-compulsive—she reminds me of that dude from that TV show *Monk*. She doesn't drink, doesn't smoke, doesn't curse, hell, she doesn't even talk. All she does is go to work and to church. Yeah, like church is gonna solve our problem. She's boring, to tell you the truth, so maybe that's why I'm drinking occasionally."

Michael leaned forward, his elbows on his thighs. "I'm not happy with my marriage, Doc. I think I married the wrong woman. Last time we had sex was six months ago. I don't find her attractive anymore. I can't even get it up with her." He leaned back again. "Shit, I can't believe I just said that. I mean, I'm a young guy. I'm still in my thirties, man; I should be having sex three times a day. I don't know, Doc, there's something wrong with my life, to tell you the truth. Maybe that's why sometimes I like to pop a xanax every now and then or have a drink or two—just to forget, to wind down, to relax, to laugh—otherwise I'll go crazy, man. She thinks I'm an alcoholic—well, compared to her, everyone is. Let me ask you something, Doc, do you drink?"

I smiled. "Let's just stay focused on you, Michael."

Michael smirked. "Okay, but I'm sure every once in a while you do have a glass of wine or something, is that a crime?"

"Do you think you're depressed?" I asked.

Michael picked at a hole in his jeans. "Depressed?" he repeated, shaking his head. "I'm not sure, Doc. I think I'm pissed. I'm angry. I'm angry at the world, because we live in a shitty world; this world is way too artificial and political. Everyone is glued to their cellphones; everyone knows everything. It is a shitty world we're living in. I mean, I should've been a CEO of a company by now. I have a master's degree and I'm a smart guy, but because we live in a fucked-up world I'm struggling to find a job. Can you believe this shit? I think I do have anger issues, but who doesn't nowadays, Doc? The economy is screwed up, people are screwed up, the world is coming to an end. Look at Charlie Sheen, Mel Gibson, Bill Cosby. Society fucked them up. Look at those who committed suicide—

and they have it all—Robin Williams, Michael Jackson, Kurt Cobain, Whitney Huston."

Our conversation continued in a similar vein.

"What the superior man seeks is in himself; what the small man seeks is in others." Confucius.

It's apparent that Michael has a problem with alcohol, but he has bigger problems too, including anger, resentment, sexual frustration, and mood problems. Michael is living in denial. Perhaps he isn't the typical alcoholic: drunk all the time, unable to wake up and go to work, unable to open his eyes without having to drink something. Maybe he doesn't drink every day, but it is apparent that alcohol lost him his job and perhaps his marriage. Whether it is alcohol dependence or alcohol abuse—whether it is cocaine dependence or cocaine abuse—it doesn't matter.

Michael has a problem with alcohol, but even bigger problems with his anger, his attitude, and his underlying misery. He's an angry, frustrated guy. He's sexually thirsty and he wants to sleep with every other woman except his wife. He feels trapped; he also feels entitled. He feels misunderstood and underappreciated. He is simply angry at himself and at the world, like a time bomb waiting to explode.

Michael will never be free unless he can become convinced that he has a problem, and this requires more than just saying it aloud. Michael must accept that the world is not the problem, that the world is not ganging up against him, that race—or what have you—is not the issue here, and that he needs to fix himself first and be honest with himself first. Otherwise, he will never get better. It doesn't matter if he is an alcoholic or not. He has a problem with alcohol—he has a problem, period—and that is enough for him to start treatment.

Honesty is the most evolved defense mechanism of all defenses, so simple yet so sophisticated, that it completes the evolutionary neuropsychological cycle of development.

Contrary to common belief, honesty is the engine that drives you and the rest of the world towards harmony. Experiencing honesty is the real high, and there is no drug in the world that comes even close to it. When people practice honesty, they evolve into a different level of being; they are no longer living in the darkness of the inferior antagonist: fear. And as Confucius put it, *"It is hard to lead with an example when you are a follower of fear."*

Fear is an inferior survival mechanism in the animal world; it is still considered an early stage in neuropsychiatric evolution. Fear is a primitive defense mechanism. Therefore, fear is the opposite of honesty. Honesty is the truth. And the truth, as we all know, shall and will always set us free.

Some of us refuse to get help because of pride or ego. In theology, pride is considered one of the seven deadly sins. Or perhaps we're thinking that we know it all and that we know what we're doing. Or perhaps we don't think that we have a serious problem, but that is because we are simply living in denial.

I hesitate to use the word "denial" in this book because it is overused and overrated, to the point that it has become a cliché. However, I must say that "denial" is actually lying; it is lying to oneself. Therefore, most people do not get help because they are lying to themselves, letting their minds play tricks on them.

One of the most popular tricks in the dictionary of the brain is, "Life is too short, too meaningless, and too boring, so I need to get high. I need to feel good." Another mind game or mind trick would be, "I can always stop if I want to." And a third one would be, "Just one more day, one more drink, one more hit, and then I'll stop."

When we surrender to the selfishness of our brains or deny that we have a problem, we are being dishonest to ourselves, to our loved ones, and to the rest of the world. We are lying to ourselves, and therefore we are sinking deeper and deeper into our inferior world of darkness; we are no longer sophisticated, honest creatures.

You might ask yourself, "What will rehab or a program do for me? What is the doctor going to do for me? I know all the answers. I know no one can help me except me. I don't need anyone to tell me what to do. I'm doing it because I want to. Plus, why should I take some medication that will make me dependent? I'm just replacing one bad habit with another. I'd rather stick with this one; at least with this one I know what I'm doing. Hell, as far as I'm concerned, marijuana is a natural, harmless plant." And in so many ways, some of that might be true. The only thing is, you are missing the point.

We are not genetically programmed to self-construction, but we are unfortunately wired for self-destruction. So if we leave it up to us—meaning up to what our brains are telling us to do, the individual, self-help approach—then we are flirting with danger, and danger in this case is our powerful brain telling us to "get lost." The brain always seeks pleasure, but obeying your brain is like following a child when you're lost in the desert: it will only lead you and the child to disaster. It is a very difficult dilemma, because there is nothing better than pleasure. After all, many of us believe that we are living in this world for pleasure, so how are we going to win this psychological battle? This is a very good question.

This is when you say to yourself, "I think I should get some help."

The most important thing in joining a program—whether it is my *3 Steps*, or 12 Steps, or any sobriety group—is "discipline," which is actually the most important word in the dictionary as far as I'm concerned, and it is the second step in *3 **Steps***. We will come to this in the next chapter of this book, and you will be astonished when you know the true meaning of the word "discipline" and its amazing applications.

You see, the minute you admit to yourself that you have a problem and you need help is the minute you've learned how to "let go" and "be free"—let go of things and accept things that are beyond your control, accept the ocean of life with its low and high waves, and learn how to avoid the tsunami. Because when you say to yourself, "I don't need help, and I don't have a problem," that's like saying you can swim against the current, when we all know it will only be a matter of time until you drown and sink to the bottom of the ocean. The ocean is too vast and powerful for you and for the rest of us.

Tzu Chang asked Confucius about Jen. Confucius said, "If you can practice these five things with all the people you can be called Jen." Tzu Chang asked what they were. Confucius said, "Courtesy, generosity, honesty, persistence, and kindness. If you are courteous, you will not be disrespected; if you are generous, you will gain everything. If you are honest, people will rely on you. If you are persistent, you will get results. If you are kind, you can employ people."

The minute you become honest and innocent, you've elevated your soul to another level of consciousness. You are no longer the bitter person you used to be; you are free. You become like a free eagle soaring high into the sky, spreading your wings wide and letting the wind taking you into a peaceful state of mind. I call it **"Way of the eagle."**

Drugs make you high in the short term, but they ultimately bring you low. And now that I'm thinking about it, heck, they should actually call it "getting low," not "getting high," because I have never met a drug addict in my life who stayed high, and neither have you; they all go from low to lower. I've treated tens of thousands of addicts from all around the world, and the message is always the same: "I'm miserable, Doc."

But what is honesty?

Honesty is not just a simple word, honesty is a commitment, a responsibility. Honesty is the hero that comes out of nowhere and save the world from doomsday. Honesty is the gravity that keeps us from floating away in a world that is full of lies and deceit; honesty is the action we take to make us look and sound different than the rest of the people around us. People will look at you and say, "She is honest, I really like her. I trust her. She is wonderful." But most importantly, honesty is the first step of recovery.

But how do we learn honesty?

Honesty with Self:

"If you look into your own heart, and you find nothing wrong there, what is there to worry about? What is there to fear?" —*Confucius*

After a week of treatment, Michael finally admitted that he did have a problem with alcohol. Even though he still didn't believe that he was an alcoholic, he admitted that there was a list of things he needed to work on and the most important one would be honesty with himself. He was put on a mood stabilizer for treatment of anger issues, and he worked on changing his attitude about life and the way he used his language.

To do this yourself, first you must start practicing immediately by being honest with yourself. You must ask yourself, "Am I being honest with myself? Do I have a problem? Do I have an addiction to a substance or to a habit? Do I have a condition that is out of control? Am I living in denial? Why am I doing this, why am I lying to myself, what should I do to redeem myself? Who am I? What am I afraid of?"

Just like learning how to play an instrument or a sport, learning honesty takes practice. You can't just sit in front of a piano, for example, and start playing unless you learn how to work the keys and then practice.

Start examining yourself until you know yourself, until you find the fear that has been eating you from the inside for years. Because once you find that fear and eliminate it, you will instantly feel relief, and you will be able to take the first move towards the first step. Remember, the journey of a thousand miles starts with one step. Know yourself. Confucius said, "The ultimate knowledge is knowing one's ignorance."

How do you find the fear in your subconscious?

Fear in the subconscious is divided into six categories:

    A. Pain fear

    B. Guilt fear

    C. Survival fear

    D. Sexual fear

    E. Fear of the unknown

    F. Fear of irrelevance

Let's start discussing each category of fear:

A. Pain Fear (Fear of pain):

1. Physical fear

2. Mental fear

3. Emotional/spiritual fear

Each and every one of us fears pain, and it is in so many ways a survival-defense mechanism embedded deeply in our DNA. It all goes back to loving one's self more than anyone or anything; we are genetically programmed in our DNA to have that kind of love, and when this love becomes an obsession or becomes overly exaggerated, we fall into the narcissism mode, which is pathological. This, of course, can lead to narcissistic personality disorder, antisocial personality, and so on.

These are all consequences of an exaggerated ego. I call it "ego obsession," which is again an exaggerated love of oneself with disregard to everyone and everything else. Ego obsession happens mostly due to the way we're brought up. As I mentioned, loving oneself is a survival mechanism, which is usually genetic. However, the act of balancing that self-love is environmental. It is an application, a learning process, that falls into teaching and family values. How was the person brought up? This is where family and environment play major roles. Because in the end, as the saying goes, "We are victims of circumstances."

The anticipation of pain is the key here, and the secret formula is to dig deep into your subconscious and find out what kind of pain you're worried about and to understand that there is no point in worrying about it. This is "self-psychology," if you will.

Dealing with pain fear can become a self-healing process, and you can control it. You might be fearing physical pain, or emotional pain, or pain of abandonment, or pain of hunger and poverty. You must find that pain and eliminate the fear that originates from it. Make it your homework for a day or two, and you will experience amazing results.

For example, let's say you have a history of sexual abuse. That by itself can cause major emotional pain, and it might live with you for the rest of your life. Many people with a history of sexual abuse start using drugs or alcohol to numb the pain and to forget. When they use drugs, they actually do forget the subconscious or the conscious pain they have, and to them, this is the perfect solution.

In reality, it is only going to make matters worse. But they don't know that, and even if they did know that, they would still do it because it gives them relief in that moment. Unless the person resolves this issue with therapy, the emotional pain will continue, and the use of drugs will not stop, not even with rehabilitation. You can go to rehabilitation for ten years, and the minute you get out, the first thing you'll do is use drugs or drink. Why? Because you never resolved this emotional pain. A good psychiatrist will help you resolve these issues, and that's why it is important to be at the right center that helps you psychologically.

B. Guilt Fear:

1. Spiritual guilt

2. Physical guilt

3. Emotional guilt

The majority of our anxiety is related to guilt, and so the question is: "Where does this guilt come from, and why?"

To answer this question, you must understand yourself first, which requires understanding your inner conflicts and desires. Guilt comes from the fact that we are a result of a complex biological and environmental system which makes us who we are. You've heard the saying, "People don't change, they just become who they are."

The environmental factors here play a major role. For example, if you believe that masturbation is wrong, then you will struggle for the rest of your life to overcome or negotiate this issue, and if for some reason you can't resolve it, then you will end up with some major anxiety which can lead you to using or experimenting with drugs.

Another example would be if you're married and you're not happy with your marriage, but you love your spouse, and you don't want to end the marriage. Let's say you end up cheating or wanting to cheat on him or her instead of facing the issue and resolving it or getting a divorce; then you'll end up with anxiety, which is guilt, and that might lead you to drink alcohol excessively and eventually become an alcoholic. Not to mention you're biologically or genetically at risk to begin with.

If you are a businessman cheating on your taxes, and you believe that doing so is wrong, then you'll end up with anxiety because deep inside you have guilt. Even if you don't feel guilty, it doesn't matter, because your subconscious knows that you're guilty and that what matters.

If you hurt someone and you know you were wrong, and you never came to terms with that person—for example, you never apologized or you never tried to do something about it, you never asked for forgiveness—then you'll have guilt anxiety. Now, if you keep doing that for a long period of time, it might lead you to the use of drugs because you want to forget the guilt, again not to mention that you're already biologically at risk.

Remember, guilt causes insomnia, because the brain is busy analyzing everything while you're trying to sleep. The brain works even when you don't want it to work; it is active twenty-four hours a day. Insomnia is a phenomenon and not an illness; it's your brain trying to tell you something.

Those internal struggles cause anxiety no matter how tough or resilient you are. To resolve the guilt anxiety, you must do the right thing first. Of course, you can never bring back the past and relive it to do it right this time around, so the best thing you can do is let go of the past and live for the future. You must come to terms with yourself first before you come to terms with the other party. Once your conscious is clear, so to speak, then you're good to go; your guilt anxiety will disappear or at least it will decline and eventually get resolved.

    C. Survival Fear:

1. Unconscious Fear (usually something you never think about)

2. Subconscious Fear (usually something you don't think about, but something that can be easily retrieved to consciousness)

3. Conscious Fear (something you always think about)

Examples of unconscious fear include fear of abandonment, anxiety itself, fear of the dark, and so on.

Examples of subconscious fear include fear of rejection, fear of abandonment, etc.

Conscious fear may be fear of hunger, thirst, physical pain, failure, etc.

But remember, the picture can be blurry, because the interconnection between these three highways is always active.

I'm sure you have heard the term "survival mechanism," if not in this book, then somewhere else. So what is a survival mechanism? Well, survival mechanisms, or "defense mechanisms," as we call them sometimes, are unconscious internal thoughts or neurological impulses in which the brain is trying to negotiate with the external world in order for it to survive (stay alive). They are brain actions trying to make sure that it (the brain or the organism) is okay and, of course, that the body that carries it is also okay.

Since the brain belongs to the body, and the body belongs to the brain, we have one complex system that interchanges information and lives as one sophisticated unit. The brain is working for you even when you're not working for it. This highly evolved and intelligent organ is fighting for survival, even when you are on vacation.

When your body is not responding, or when your brain conceives that you're not fit for survival, it tends to let you know, and when it does, you develop anxiety. That is the exact origin of "survival anxiety." Remember, anxiety is fear, and fear causes anxiety. You can't have one without the other.

Let me give you an example. Let's say you're not exercising, or you just sit on your ass all day, eating, drinking, smoking, and using drugs. Then your brain will start to analyze the situation even when you don't want to analyze it. It works regardless of whether you want it to or not; it is out of your control. Your brain works independently, and by doing so, it sends you messages.

These messages might travel from the unconscious to the subconscious and eventually to the conscious…back and forth. Your brain lets you know that you're not doing the right thing and that you need to stop doing what you're doing. It tells you that you will die soon if you keep doing what you're doing; in fact it might even flash the word "death," and whether you like it or not, now you become anxious and might even end up having a panic attack. Therefore, panic attacks come from survival fear (survival anxiety), meaning your brain is telling you "You're going to die, you're going to die." To solve this problem, first you must understand this phenomenon, and second, you must start doing the right thing.

Once you start doing the right thing—for example, stop using drugs, start exercising, stop doing risky behaviors—then your panic attacks will eventually disappear.

D. Sexual Fear:

Sexual fear is divided into three categories:

1. Fear of castration

2. Fear of deprivation

3. Fear of destruction

Let's discuss each one:

1. Fear of Castration (Castration Anxiety):

Sexual fear in women is different from sexual fear in men. Sexual fear in men originates mostly from "castration anxiety." This castration anxiety exists in women also, but it has different manifestations and connotations. For example, castration anxiety in women is connected to childbearing and the fact that females have a specific period of time for childbearing (fertility), from adolescence to menopause. Whereas in men, castration anxiety is mostly related to performance, which actually makes perfect sense; after all, it is a biological issue more than just a psychological one.

Men in general have subconscious fear of becoming castrated physically or psychologically, meaning they struggle with their inner anxiety in regard to their sexual performance with a partner or partners. Of course, in the animal kingdom, including humans, the role of males is to impregnate as many females as possible in order to ensure the transfer or the continuation of their genes—and the information those genes contain—to the next generation. I call it "information preservation;" this is the concept of immortality, after all, because all of us are mortal unless we transfer our genes to the next generation. Only then do we become immortal. This is not a "Dracula concept," but a scientific and biological concept.

2. Fear of Sexual Deprivation (Deprivation Anxiety):

The majority of men suffer from "sexual obsession," which varies in degree depending on genetic makeup and environmental impact. Even though the majority of males deny sexual obsession, and they have all the right to do so, the reality of it is obvious and practical in our society. All you have to do is look at sexual crimes and you'll find that more than 99.9% of them are committed by men from different educational and cultural backgrounds.

Men subconsciously seek sex twenty-four hours a day until the day they expire, regardless of whether they can perform or not. They are genetically programmed this way; it has nothing to do with morality or performance, it is simply instinctual. So the lack of multiple partners (since multiple partners are unaccepted in most societies) can cause deprivation anxiety. Nevertheless, training and discipline, which is the whole mark of a civilization, may decrease that anxiety to an acceptable level, and so the environment in this case is the key factor in shaping the individual.

In women, "deprivation anxiety" is also a factor, but to a lesser extent. The concept of deprivation anxiety in women is different, because in females it is simply related to sexual satisfaction, which can be achieved with one partner and not necessarily multiple sexual partners. Again, females have an emotional component added to the sexual component; they are simply more sophisticated and more evolved psycho-biologically, but not necessarily physically. And that, I might add, makes perfect sense biologically and evolutionarily.

The other issue with deprivation anxiety is the fact that males continue their journey in life searching for sexual compatibility, which might become a lifelong battle even if the person is married or has a permanent partner. The issue is more psychological than actual. Most people live for the fantasy and not necessary for the action. Humans are in love with fantasies—the fantasy of the object and not necessarily the object itself. I call this phenomenon—which is unique to humans— "object fantasy."

3. Fear of Sexual Destruction (Destruction Anxiety):

The other issue is "sexual identity crisis" in regard to sexual orientation. Many heterosexuals might have desires for the same sex, but since they are mostly heterosexual, this can create sexual anxiety, and that can lead to depression and other pathological issues. It all goes back to the impact of the environment on the individual.

Even if the person is homosexual and has no interest in the opposite sex, still anxiety will always be an important factor, perhaps because homosexuals are equipped neither physically nor psychologically with the right tools, if I may, to conduct sexual activities with the same sex; it is simply unnatural. (And when I say unnatural, I don't mean abnormal; I mean that the action itself does not produce results for the continuation of a species, meaning there is no egg fertilization.)

However, homosexuality has been accepted—and rightfully so—in most modern societies as personal preference and personal freedom, and therefore homosexual anxiety is a "culture-bound phenomenon," meaning its intensity can vary from society to society or from country to county, depending on acceptability. This kind of sexual fear originates from destruction anxiety, meaning the damage that is done to the fragile ego can lead to anxiety and depression along with other psychiatric illnesses and conditions such as drug use.

In women, sexual identity is extremely fragile because it has a strong emotional component; therefore, sexual assault or harassment or sexual abuse such as rape can cause some serious damage to the psyche of females, and that can lead to serious mental health issues and substance abuse. Even verbal assault or psychological assault can cause some serious destruction to the fragile female ego. Sexual abuse both in men and women is catastrophic. In fact, the majority of mental illnesses originate from drug use and sexual abuse in both men and women, and this has been proven beyond the shadow of a doubt.

E. Fear of the Unknown (Fear of Uncertainty):

Every one of us has fear of the unknown. Fear of the unknown is divided into three categories: fear of the future, fear of the past, and fear of death.

1. Fear of the Future:

"Never worry about tomorrow, for tomorrow will worry about itself." —Matthew 6:34

No matter how tough you think you are, deep inside your subconscious, you have fear of the future: not knowing where you're going, not knowing what is going to happen to you, wondering if you will lose your job, your health, your youth, your loved ones, your parents, your mind, and wondering when you will die (which we will explore further in the next chapter).

The issue might not seem like an emergency, but subconsciously, it is. Anxiety strikes with no warning, and that is why people with panic attacks always claim, "I have no idea why I had a panic attack. I mean, it makes no sense to me at all. Why would I have a panic attack all of the sudden?" But in reality, it does make perfect sense, because when you analyze the person and find out their most intimate fears, you'll know why they had panic attacks.

That, of course, must be resolved too, because anxiety can lead to depression and to substance abuse or continuation and relapse of substance abuse. You must extract that fear and accept the future. Accept the unknown as a good thing, not a bad thing. Positivity is the key word here; being negative is only going to bring you more anxiety and more problems. So having a future and having faith in the future is in fact a good thing. We must always remember that whatever happens to us is natural, and we are all going through it together. The future does not discriminate against anyone; the future belongs to all of us and we should respect it, accept it, and embrace it.

2. Fear of the Past:

"Let the dead bury their dead." —Jesus.

The past is gone, even though there is no future without it. The past is forgiving, and so you should be forgiving, too. We have all done stupid and ugly things in our past, and no one in this world is perfect; however, most of us are still living in the past. Most of us still dwell on the ugly things we've done and the wrong decisions we've made. This can cause major anxiety and depression, which in turn can lead to substance abuse and maladaptive behaviors.

It's funny how a simple, uneducated client of mine taught me a lesson in psychology. He said, "Anxiety is worrying about the future, and depression is worrying about the past."

In so many words, he's right. There is no point living in the past. Learn from the past and move on; unless you move on and let go, you will never be free.

3. Fear of Death:

"If we don't know life, how can we know death?" — **Confucius**

This is again an unconscious and subconscious phenomenon. Most of us don't walk around thinking consciously about death all day long, but it is embedded in us, and can become more present when we get sick or age. Many people have some serious planning in their lives for when they're alive and when they're long gone. I'm talking financial planning, a will, and life insurance. Some people are wealthy, and they worry about what is going to happen to them when they die and what they are going to do with their money. I know some of you might be thinking, "I wish I had that kind of worry," but believe me, even if you have little money, you still might worry about what will happen to your assets should something happen to you.

Most people also worry about what will happen to them when they die. Are they just going to vanish forever? Religious people worry about heaven and hell. For unreligious people it's even worse, because at least religious people see it as a fifty-fifty chance, but for people who don't believe in anything, the odds are much worse, at least to them. So, in order for you to live a peaceful happy life, you must believe in something.

As we know, science has proven that we are part of a complex unit, part of the universe, and nothing disappears. Even if you don't believe in God or life after death, you must still believe that you're not going to disappear forever. At least your energy is going to be preserved—the energy which some people call the soul or the spirit—and it is going to be around eternally. That should make you feel better, because when you do the right thing or at least when you try to do the right thing, you'll feel good about yourself. So there is no reason for anyone to fear death, because death is still part of life, and no matter what, you will not go to a bad place after you die, because God, if you believe in God, is forgiving and ever-loving. The issue is not for God to forgive you, the issue is for you to forgive yourself.

F. Fear of Irrelevance (Vanity Anxiety):

"Worry not that no one knows of you; seek to be worth knowing." —Confucius

The fear of irrelevance or vanity is unique to humans; they don't want to leave this world without leaving their mark on it, and some are willing to cross the line just to achieve recognition. People don't want to be irrelevant in their lives, and that's why addiction to fame is a big problem in modern societies, especially with the explosion of reality TV and social media. People are willing to do anything and everything to be on TV; some are willing to expose their most intimate and personal matters for the sake of money or fame.

But even thousands of years ago, before there was anything called media, vanity was a significant issue in our lives, and it still is today. Unless we free ourselves from the chains of vanity, we will never be free. After all, what is the point of winning the world and losing your soul? The right approach would be to actually keep a low profile and do the right thing; if you do this, you will be rewarded and you will be known—not necessarily by the entire world, but by your close friends and the people who really know you, the ones that matter.

Sometimes we cross the line in our lives just to be pointed at, just to be known, to announce to the rest, "Hey, I'm here." But that should be the last thing on our agenda. This fear of irrelevance comes from the fragile ego; its exaggeration can lead to narcissism and antisocial personality, which in turn can lead to substance abuse. So the solution would be to know yourself and rearrange your priorities in life.

After you perform radical surgery on your inner self and find and extract lies out of your subconscious, you have conquered the living fear inside you—because remember, your ultimate enemy is fear itself. Only then will your wings start to grow, and you will eventually take off.

You must start by forgiving yourself first, because forgiving oneself is the beginning of this beautiful and amazing journey. Once you've done that, you have taken the first move towards the first step of recovery.

Look at yourself in the mirror. Look at yourself in the eye. Talk to yourself, and carry on a serious conversation with yourself: "I'm so sorry because I've been lying to you all these years. I've treated you with deceit and disrespect. I've neglected you, and I am asking for your forgiveness. I am not perfect, but I promise you from now on that I will be honest and sincere with you, and I will always treat you with love, respect, and dignity, no matter what. You can depend on me from now on. I love you." This is when tears of joy start pouring down your cheeks, and you know you're about to conquer your worst enemy: your own fear.

After you complete the self-cleansing process and get rid of the poison of years of lies and deceit, and after you have forgiven yourself for all the negative ways you've impacted your health and your life…only then you can make the second move.

Honesty with the Loved Ones:

"The least initial deviation from the truth is multiplied later a thousandfold." —Aristotle

Become honest with your family. Start with the people closest to you: your husband or your wife if you're married, then your children if you have children, and then your mother and your father if they are still alive. If one of them has passed away, you will go to the flower shop, buy some flowers—pretty ones—and take a trip to the cemetery. You will kneel down and ask for their forgiveness. You will tell them how much pain you've caused them, how you've lied to them over and over again, and how much you love them and how sorry you are. You will promise them that you will not lie again. And after you say your prayers, you may pause and reflect upon yourself and then send them a big smile, because they have already forgiven you.

Next, be honest with your siblings, your boyfriend or girlfriend, and your best friends. You need to tell them how sorry you are, that you are working to improve yourself, and that you are taking the first step of recovery—learning how to be honest—and that it will take time.

You will confess to your loved ones the lies you've told them just to feed your addiction. Or, if you don't have an addiction (or you think you don't have an addiction), then it is about your condition. It does not really matter what you're suffering from, because *3 Steps* works for every condition; it will cleanse you from all the poisonous psychological chemicals you've been accumulating throughout the years.

It is irrelevant at this point if people forgive you or not, though they will; it does not matter what the world thinks of you, it only matters that you've come clean with yourself. Then and only then you can sleep comfortably in your bed without nightmares or insomnia. Unless you come clean, your night terrors will continue to haunt you for the rest of your life, because living with lies is the worst feeling in the world. Lies will make you feel guilty, because guilt comes mostly from living a dishonest life. When you conquer your fear, you cross over to the other side where the grass is green and the sky is blue. There, you can see the rainbow.

With honesty, you will influence people around you. Your friends will start saying things about you. "What happened to Jack? He is so different. He seems happy. He looks so peaceful." They will think that you know something they don't, and they'll want to be just like you. They'll want to know your secret. Even though in the beginning they might've called you a douchebag or some other names, later on down the road you will become their hero.

But remember, you're not doing this for them; you are doing it for yourself. You will never feel free unless you free yourself. In fact, you should never take the road to recovery for anyone but yourself. Because if the horse is sick, the jockey will never win the race, and you are the horse of this race. You are the captain of your ship.

Honesty with the Universe:

"Natural forces within us are the true healers of disease."
—Hippocrates (460–370 BC)

You might ask, "How the hell am I going to be honest with the universe?" It's simple. First of all, you must realize that you are part of this universe, connected to it in every micro-molecule, all the way to the origin of matter—in fact, all the way to the origin of energy. Science has already proven it without a shadow of a doubt, so this is not just philosophy, this is the law of physics. And so when you do something, even if no one sees you or knows about it—or so you think—the universe has its eyes on you.

You are constantly being watched and ranked by the universe, not by cameras, but by the invisible eyes of electrons, protons, bacteria, fungus, viruses, and the DNA that is floating in the air all around you. In fact, you are watching yourself.

When you do something behind closed doors and you assume that no one knows, no one sees, or that you're not hurting anyone, you're forgetting that you are actually being watched by yourself. Even if you were blind, it wouldn't matter; the plant in your room, the fly on your window, the air you breathe, they are all watching you. Now, I don't want to make you paranoid. You know what they say: "A little paranoia is good, too much of it is bad."

But in the end, you are part of a highly sophisticated system. You are connected to the rest of the world. Like it or not, you can't exist individually in this world, because the ultimate laws of the universe never work individually, and nothing exists individually. You are part of a simple yet complicated system. You are the universe. The forces within you are the universe.

When you destroy your life with drugs, you are being selfish, because you are not only destroying your life but the universe, the lives of millions of people in the world, who are part of the universe. How?

Well, when you use drugs of abuse, for example, someone will copy you because you copied someone else to begin with, and so ultimately, you have negatively affected millions of people around the world. If you don't know the meaning of God, or you don't believe in God, and that is fine too, well, this concept is God to you.

When you cut a tree, for example, thinking, "It is making my backyard dirty," you are affecting the amount of oxygen in the air around and inside your house, in your area, in your city, in your state, in your country, in the world and eventually in the universe, and therefore the universe will certainly retaliate; it is the law of physics and it is always accurate. It will come back to you.

So never say to yourself, "But I'm only hurting myself," or "But no one can see me," or "It's a white lie." There is no such thing as a white lie. A lie is a lie, and when you lie to yourself, you are lying to the entire universe.

But I guess the question is, what's this got to do with addiction or recovery? Well, everything. Because when you are dishonest with the universe, you're trying to change the laws of the universe, which are perfect and unchangeable. Therefore, bad things will happen to you, because the universe will change you, and so eventually those bad things will lead you back to drugs. You know what they say: "Everything is connected to everything."

People start using drugs for many different reasons. The cause is irrelevant, but the effect is always the same.

People continue to use drugs because they are miserable. They are dishonest, and that is why they are miserable. That is why honesty is the first step of recovery, and without it, there will be no recovery. There will be no freedom.

Even if you never suffered from addiction to a substance, honesty is still the all-important first step in your life: the first step to life, the first step to freedom. Because only the truth will set you free.

Chapter Two

Discipline

"When I let go of what I am, I become what I might be"
Lao Tzu 601 B.C.

Larissa, a seventeen-year-old girl whose father is a famous actor in Hollywood, told me, "Doc, I don't think I can make it here. I just love drugs, to be honest with you. Just thinking that I'm never gonna use drugs again, like ever again, is just like mind-boggling to me, you know what I mean? I'm never gonna use mushrooms or ecstasy at a party? Are you shitting me? It's no fun. It's just no fun. 'Never' is just not an option for me, Doc. I mean, honestly, my mom wants me to be here. I don't think my dad knows, and I know I have a problem with drugs, but for some reason I don't think of it like they do.

"You know, I think I will actually be very depressed if I don't use drugs. I know it sounds like…strange to you and stuff, but I'm not motivated to get off drugs. I'm not." Then she asked me for a cigarette.

"I don't have one," I said. "I don't smoke."

"Good for you," she added.

"OK, so you seem like a smart guy," she said. "Where are you from, anyway? I like your accent. Actually, it doesn't matter. You seem like a cool dude. I'm sure you used drugs when you were my age, and plus, how can you treat someone who is unmotivated, Doc?

"I mean, think about it. I'm not saying it's right. I'm not saying I don't get into trouble in school and stuff, but come on, I'm young and I want to have fun in my life. My dad is busy making movies. I hardly see him, and he and my mom don't even talk. I think they're getting a divorce or something, but I don't really care. She has her life, he has his life, and I have mine. My mom has a boyfriend, alright? Can you test me for HIV and STD's and stuff? By the way, I hope everything I tell you is confidential."

"Yes, it is," I assured her.

So the second thing Larissa needs to learn—after learning honesty, of course—is discipline, and as we can clearly see, there is no discipline in her life.

"The first and the best victory is to conquer self" —Plato (424–348 BC)

Now, when I say discipline, I'm not referring to "the will." Because most of us don't have "the will," but all of us can acquire discipline. There is a significant difference between *discipline* and *will*. For example, most of us might not have *the will* to quit drinking, smoking, or binging, but we can do it by taking it one day at a time, by applying the simple act of discipline. You must become like a samurai warrior who lives by the "Way of the Samurai."

A samurai warrior in ancient Japan who lives by **Bushido**, "Way of the Warrior," will discipline himself by not being hasty in taking actions, even when provoked by someone he's certain he could cut in half in a split second with his Katana sword. Because of the concept of discipline, he prevents himself from this violence. He replaces anger and impulse with self-control, and by doing so, he saves two lives: his and his opponent's.

You must discipline yourself at the specific moment of weakness to purposely act—or not act—in order to NOT satisfy your desires but to satisfy the order of the universe. Succumbing to the lust of your desires will only lead you to destruction.

Here are the eight virtues of the Bushido code:

1. ***Righteousness gi***

   "If there's righteousness in the heart, there will be beauty in the character. If there is beauty in the character there will be harmony in the home. If there is harmony in the home, there will be order in the nation. If there is order in the nation, there will be peace in the world." -Confucius.

   This is the quality of being morally correct and just. "It can also be considered synonymous with 'rightness'. It is also a concept that can be found in Dharmic traditions and Abrahamic traditions as a theological concept. For example, from various perspectives in Hinduism, Christianity, and Judaism, it is considered an attribute that implies that a person's actions are justified, and can have the connotation that the person has been 'judged' or 'reckoned' as leading a just life that is pleasing to God."

For the samurai warrior, to be righteous is to be acutely honest throughout your dealings with all people. Believe in justice, not from other people, but from yourself. To the true warrior, all points of view are deeply considered regarding honesty, justice, and integrity. Warriors make a full commitment to their decisions.

2. Heroic Courage *yu*

Hiding like a turtle in a shell is not living at all. A true warrior must have heroic courage. It is absolutely risky. It is living life completely, fully, and wonderfully. Heroic courage is not blind. It is intelligent and strong.

3. Benevolence, Compassion *jin*

Through intense training and hard work, the true warrior becomes quick and strong. They are not as most people. They develop a power that must be used for good. They have compassion. They help their fellow men at every opportunity. If an opportunity does not arise, they go out of their way to find one.

4. *Respect Rei*

True warriors have no reason to be cruel. They do not need to prove their strength. Warriors are not only respected for their strength in battle, but also by their dealings with others. The true strength of a warrior becomes apparent during difficult times.

5. *Honesty makoto*

When warriors say that they will perform an action, it is as good as done. Nothing will stop them from completing what they say they will do. They do not have to 'give their word'. They do not have to 'promise'. Speaking and doing are the same action.

6. *Honor meiyo*

Warriors have only one judge of honor and character, and this is themselves. Decisions they make and how these decisions are carried out are a reflection of who they truly are. You cannot hide from yourself.

7. Duty and Loyalty Chugi

Warriors are responsible for everything that they have done and everything that they have said and all of the consequences that follow. They are immensely loyal to all of those in their care. To everyone that they are responsible for, they remain fiercely true.

8. Self-Control jisei

Self-Control, an aspect of inhibitory control, is the ability to regulate one's emotions, thoughts, and behavior in the face of temptations and impulses. As an executive function, self-control is a cognitive process that is necessary for regulating one's behavior in order to achieve specific goals. A related concept in psychology is emotional self-regulation. Self-control is like a muscle. According to studies, self-regulation, whether emotional or behavioral, was proven to be a limited resource which functions like energy. In the short term, overuse of self-control will lead to depletion. However, in the long term, the use of self-control can strengthen and improve over time.

Will is perhaps genetic. Either you have it, or you don't. But discipline is a learning process. Therefore, you must teach yourself and train your heart in the art of discipline. Just like the first step, the second step has three moves.

Discipline Your Mind:

"The mark of an educated mind is entertaining an idea without accepting it." —Aristotle

"Discipline my mind, are you crazy, Doc? Are you, like, high on something? Because this shit is too deep for me."

This was Larissa's comment on disciplining the mind.

"How the fuck am I going to discipline my mind?" she asked. "What does that mean?"

Contrary to common belief, discipline is not punishment. Discipline is a way of life. It takes practice to learn discipline.

When your mind is telling you to do something harmful that seems like a good idea in the moment, you are having an intimate conversation with your mind. Acknowledge this intimate conversation, and tell your mind, "I will pass on this for now." The *now* impulse is replaced by the concept of *later*.

The mind is a powerful thing, but it is open to suggestions. It is highly evolved and extremely flexible, therefore you can negotiate with it. This concept is called **"self-psychology."**

For example, let's say you are an alcoholic at a party with a bunch of people drinking alcohol, or doing Ecstasy. You are tempted. Your mind is telling you, "You can just have one drink or do one hit and then stop. What's the big deal?"

But because you're teaching your mind discipline, you tell your mind to back off; you prevent yourself from taking that first drink. Instead, you say to yourself, "I am not going to take that drink today, because I am disciplining my mind. Instead I'm going to drink this entire bottle of water." And then you say, "Let me see what happens to me today if I don't do it. Let me experiment on myself."

You don't think about tomorrow. Tomorrow is just another day, and you are taking it one move at a time. You tell your mind, "I am not stopping drinking forever, but I am training you today. I am training you now."

Discipline does not have to be eternal. When it comes to addiction, it is a scary thought to many addicts to know that they must abstain from drinks or drugs forever. The word "forever" is a scary word, and thinking this way is risky, because too much fear can lead to relapse, just like an increase in anxiety can lead to a decrease in performance. You've heard the saying, "A little anxiety is good; too much of it is bad." The key is to focus on one move, one day, at a time.

All great things in life start with small steps, small moves, and your long journey to freedom starts with one little step.

Some addiction centers—or some people, I should say—might say, "One hour at a time." It sounds impressive, but this is not the best strategy, because one hour at a time can also cause anxiety, just like one year at a time. Focus on one day at a time, because a day represents a new beginning. You sleep it off; the next day you wake up fresh and clean and feeling good about yourself.

Discipline Your Body:

"We are what we repeatedly do, excellence then is not an act, but a habit." —Aristotle

1. Healthy nutritional habits
2. Exercise
3. Stopping the vicious cycle

How do we teach ourselves discipline of the body?

The samurai warrior learns discipline by going to school, joining a program, and having a mentor (a master).

The master must give the student physical and mental homework. The physical homework consists of:

1. How and what to ingest.
2. How and when to speak.

3. How and when to exercise.

4. How and when to react.

The same thing goes for the addict or anyone with a bad habit. Even if you don't think you have an addiction, discipline is one of the most important qualities you can learn. It is not only going to help us conquer addiction, it will also help us live a happy life and deal with daily challenges. Unfortunately, most of us do not apply this simple principle.

Way of the Samurai:

Consider the tale of the monk and the Samurai warrior:

Once upon a time, there was a Samurai warrior who decided to leave his master in the castle and become a *ronin* (drifter). He decided to find the meaning of life, and so he traveled a thousand miles to reach the mountains.

There he was told about a solitary monk with a great reputation for wisdom. The samurai decided to meet the monk, but the monk refused because he could only meet one person every year, and so the warrior waited his turn.

Five years later, the monk agreed to meet the samurai warrior. The samurai warrior was relieved and very happy to finally meet the monk so he could learn the meaning of life, but when the samurai warrior asked the monk, the monk told him regretfully that he couldn't teach him the meaning of life. The Monk told the samurai that he should pack and leave.

The warrior was very disappointed and asked the monk for an explanation. The monk told him that although he was one hundred years old, he still could not understand the full meaning of life. However, the monk saw that the samurai was serious and devoted to his cause, so he offered to teach him something about himself in three years. The samurai accepted the offer.

The monk said to the samurai, "You must follow the rules. There are only two rules. Rule number one: you must do your homework, no questions asked. Rule number two: you shall never speak to me, or speak, period, for the entire three years."

The samurai asked the monk, "What is my homework?"

The monk said, "It is simple, my son. Every morning, you take this empty bucket and fill it up with water from the stream down the hill and bring it up here and empty it in this big hole. Your other homework is that every afternoon I will give you one word and you have to copy it and write it on the floor until you fill this entire section."

The samurai asked, "When do I start?"

The monk answered, "You will start your journey tomorrow morning." And so the samurai accepted the deal.

Every morning, the samurai would take the bucket and fill it up with water from the stream and walk all the way up the hill and empty it into the large hole in the ground. After lunch, he would start his second homework, which was to copy the word given to him by the monk. And sure enough, he would do that for the rest of the afternoon until sunset. The samurai continued his homework for three years and never dared to open his mouth

After exactly three years, the samurai completed his work and decided to leave and go back to town. Before he left, he saw the monk meditating on the top of the mountain. So the Samurai waited until the monk finished his meditation. The monk understood that the three years were over and the vow of silence could be broken on that day.

The monk walked to the hole where the samurai had poured all that water for the entire three years. By now, the hole was filled all the way to the top. The monk opened a gate that was connected to the hole, and all the water gushed back to the stream where it came from. The samurai was shocked, wondering why the monk had done that. But still, he didn't dare to open his mouth.

The monk walked to the spot where the samurai had written millions of copies of the words given to him by the monk and asked the samurai to erase them all. The samurai was in shock and did not know what to say, but he did what the monk asked him to do. And still, he never dared to ask why.

At last the monk gave the samurai warrior permission to speak, and so naturally the samurai asked, "Master, why did you empty the hole I filled for all those years back to the river?"

The monk smiled and said, "Because the hole fulfilled its purpose, my son."

The samurai asked, "Master, why did you make me erase all the words I copied all those years?"

And the monk smiled again and said, "Because the words fulfilled their purpose, my son."

The samurai asked, "Master, what was the purpose of filling the hole with water?"

The monk answered, "Discipline, my son."

The samurai asked, "Master, what was the purpose of copying all those words for all those years?"

The monk answered, "Discipline, my son."

The samurai suddenly smiled and said, "Now I understand, master, thank you."

The monk replied, "Go to the world, my son; now you know a little something about yourself."

The wise monk prayed over him, and the samurai warrior walked away into the horizon with a big smile on his face.

Way of the Samurai:

Three Lessons

1. You must know, understand, and judge yourself before you try to know, understand, and judge others.

2. You must not be hasty or impulsive in your reaction to situations. You must count to 10 before you react internally or externally to any situation. For example, if there is a person in front of you and he or she is provoking you or insulting you, you must understand that this person is not doing it because *you* have a problem, but because *he* or *she* has a problem. And their reaction is not personal. Also you must know that "anger kills the angry."

3. Before you react, you must separate yourself from your emotions. You must take a deep breath and believe that being calm, cool, and collected is going to give you the advantage in a given situation. When you act, you must understand the ultimate law of the universe: "For every action, there is a reaction." Therefore, sometimes the best action is no action. You must appreciate the value of silence.

"Silence is the true friend that never betrays you." — Confucius

You must conquer your current desire in the current situation. Your desire might be to take action, such as chopping off the head of the person standing in front of you, or cursing at him or her, or hitting him or her, because he or she angered you. But you are not going to do that, because chopping his head off will lead to your head being chopped off eventually. It is the law of the universe, and there is no way out of it. You must always remember that "he or she who angers you controls you."

Now, let's apply this principle in our lives. Let's apply this principle in the treatment of addiction, anger, anxiety, or obesity.

It is very simple, but we must practice it, just like practicing playing the guitar or playing soccer. We can never perfect our lives unless we practice. Please do understand that we are not trying to live a perfect life; no one can. But we must always seek to elevate ourselves so we can live in harmony with people around us, with the world, and with the universe.

Discipline Your Soul:

"What good does it do to you to gain the whole world but lose your soul?" —Jesus

Ancient Egyptians believed that the soul consists of five parts.

One important part—thought to be the heart—is ***the ib***. The *ib* was believed to be formed from one drop of blood from the child's mother's heart, taken at conception. To ancient Egyptians, it was the heart and not the brain that was the seat of emotion, thought, will, and intention. This is evidenced by the many expressions in the Egyptian language that incorporate the word *ib*, such as *Awt-ib*, which means happiness.

"Into men's heart, I looked by my wisdom, found them not free from the bondage of strife. Free from the toils, thy fire, oh my brother! Lest it be buried in the shadow of night." –The Egyptian God Thoth.

In Egyptian religion, the heart was also the key to the afterlife. It was perceived as surviving death in the netherworld, where it gave evidence for, or against, its possessor. It was thought that the heart was examined by Anubis and the deities during the *Weighing of the Heart* ceremony. If the heart weighed more than the *feather of Maat*, it was immediately consumed by the monster Ammit.

The second part of the soul in the ancient Egyptian view is **the Shadow**. A person's shadow, **Sheut,** was always present. It was believed that a person could not exist without a shadow, nor a shadow without a person, therefore, Egyptians surmised that a shadow contained something of the person it represented. For this reason, statues of people and deities were sometimes referred to as their shadows. The shadow was represented graphically as a small human figure painted completely black, as well as a figure of death, or servant of Anubis.

The third part was **The Name (Ren).** As a part of the soul, a person's *ren* was given to him or her at birth and the Egyptians believed that it would live for as long as that name was spoken, which explains why efforts were made to protect it and the practice of placing it in numerous writings. For example, part of the *Book of Breathings*, a derivative of the *Book of the Dead*, was a means to ensure the survival of the name. A cartouche (magical rope) often was used to surround the name and protect it.

Conversely, the names of deceased enemies of the state, such as Akhenaten, were hacked out of monuments in a form of *damnatio memoriae*. The greater the number of places a name was used, the greater the possibility it would survive to be read and spoken.

The fourth part is Soul, **the 'Ba'**. The 'Ba' is in some regards the closest to the contemporary Western religious notion of a *soul*, but it also was everything that makes an individual unique, similar to the notion of 'personality'. (In this sense, inanimate objects could also have a 'Ba', a unique character, and indeed Old Kingdom pyramids often were called the 'Ba' of their owner.) Like a soul, the 'Ba' is an aspect of a person that the Egyptians believed would live after the body died, and it is sometimes depicted as a human-headed bird flying out of the tomb to join with the *ka* in the afterlife.

    The fifth part is ***ka (vital spark)***, the Egyptian concept of vital essence, that which distinguishes the difference between a living and a dead person, with death occurring when the *ka* left the body. The Egyptians believed that Khnum created the bodies of children on a potter's wheel and inserted them into their mothers' bodies. Depending on the region, Egyptians believed that Heket or Meskhenet was the creator of each person's *ka*, breathing it into them at the instant of their birth as the part of their soul that made them alive. This resembles the concept of spirit in other religions.

You don't have to believe in God or to belong to a religion to know that the soul is an important part of your life. It's been said by the ancients: *"He who lives without a soul, lives without a life."*

"The superior man loves his soul; the inferior man loves his property." - Confucius.

Your soul is part of your inner self that actually doesn't belong just to you, but to the universe. Your soul is not for you to keep; you don't own it. It's been leased for your body, for you. It is for you to share. You have borrowed it from the universe and now it is up to you to discipline it, to keep it safe and clean, to stop it from wandering in the wrong direction. You must protect your soul so it can protect you. You can't ignore your soul and expect it to keep you happy; you must respect your soul, that inner part of you that believes in something, that inner part of you that believes that tomorrow is going to be a better day, that you are significant even if no one knows who you are.

"I am not bothered by the fact that I am unknown, I am bothered if I don't know others." —Confucius

You must believe in your soul, in yourself, in order for your soul to trust you. This is also part of the ultimate law of the universe, "For every action there is a reaction."

So the priceless question is, what is the soul, really?

The soul, according to Wikipedia, is "the incorporeal and immortal essence of a person, living thing, or object."

Whatever the soul might be, it is those principles which you live by that make up your soul, the truth within you that makes you do the right thing and that believes in you. Your soul is part of the whole; you are not just matter, you don't just live and die and disappear forever or have no effect on the world, because each and every one of us has a great impact on every living and nonliving thing in the universe.

You are not alone. You are part of us, and we are part of you. Unless you believe in this concept, in this reality, then you are missing your potential, the greatness in you. Because there is greatness in each and every one of us.

But how do you really discipline your soul?

It is actually simple: first you must believe that you have one. Then you must believe in yourself, and believe that your inner desires come from somewhere within you. You must know that you will never reach perfection, but at least you should try. Deep inside you, you must know that doing the right thing in life can be difficult sometimes, but you should believe that when you do it, you will be greatly rewarded for it. And finally, you must conquer your desires.

For example, let's say you suffer from addiction to a drug or from a condition. If you don't believe that you have a soul (something other than the physical, material world around you), then you are living an empty, meaningless life, and you will eventually succumb to addiction to fill the emptiness within you. Therefore, you must believe in something. You must believe that your life is not going to expire just like that and then you disappear. You must believe that the impact of your life in this world is actually eternal, because your soul is eternal, because you are part of this amazing universe that is eternal.

This has nothing to do with religion; this is physics. In quantum physics, things don't just disappear; energy is matter and matter is energy.

"Birth is not the begging of life – only of individual awareness. Change into another state is not death – only the ending of this awareness." –Thoth.

Remember, we are all connected, and whatever you do in this life will have an impact on you and everyone and everything else in the universe forever. Therefore, you must discipline your soul; you must know that doing the right thing is the right thing to do, and doing the wrong thing is the wrong thing to do. Remember, do good and you'll receive good, do bad and you'll receive bad. Call it karma, call it whatever you'd like to call it. This is not philosophy, this is physics; this is science and this is the truth.

By disciplining your soul, you are telling yourself, "I must do the right thing, not just for my body, but for my soul. I can't be selfish, and therefore I must respect my soul so it doesn't wander in the wrong direction." It is all about training.

Nowadays, almost every celebrity in Hollywood has some story about souls or ghosts they encounter in their lives. In fact, there is a show on TV called *Celebrity Ghost Stories*, and it seems that unless you believe in that energy within you, you don't become a celebrity, you don't reach your potential.

Whether you believe in ghosts or not, that's not the point; the point is that the energy of the people stays there long after they're gone, because in reality they are never gone. Their souls are never gone.

Einstein and other scientists have proven that matter is interchangeable with energy, so it is simply impossible for any one of us not to have a soul, because that is the energy within us. We must train that energy not to be used in the wrong way. That is called "disciplining your soul."

Before you do something by simply obeying your desires, discipline your soul. This way you won't accept bad habits, like using drugs, because you want to prevent bad things from happening. This is why you need to train your soul: to prevent you from falling into the deep, black hole. Even the universe has a black hole that sucks the stars into it, and in reality, unless the universe itself had discipline it wouldn't exist to begin with.

By not doing something harmful to your life and to the people around you, you are disciplining your soul, and in return your soul will reward you. It will protect you, it will keep you alive, and it will bring you happiness.

Chapter Three

Change

"They must often change who would be constant in happiness and wisdom." —Confucius

I'd like to tell you a story about Change, the frog that lived in a shallow well.

"Look how well-off I am here!" he told a big turtle from the Eastern Ocean. "I can hop along the edge of the well when I go out and rest by a crevice in the bricks when I return. I can wallow to my heart's content with only my head above water, or stroll toe deep through soft mud. No crabs or tadpoles can compare with me. I am master of the water and lord of this shallow well. What more can a fellow ask? Why don't you come here more often to have a good time?"

Before the turtle from the Eastern Ocean could get his left foot into the well, however, he caught his right claw on something. So he halted and stepped back. Then he began to describe the ocean to the frog.

"It's more than a thousand miles across and more than ten thousand feet deep," said the Turtle. "In ancient times, there were floods nine years out of ten, yet the water in the ocean never increased.

"And later, there were droughts seven years out of eight, yet the water in the ocean never grew less. It has remained quite constant throughout the ages. That is why I like to live in the Eastern Ocean."

The frog teaches us that everyone can find a reason for why they shouldn't leave their environment or change their lifestyle.

Now you have come clean with yourself and others, and now you have taught yourself the secrets of discipline. You went to the battle, and you came out bruised but uninjured. You came out a winner. You finished your program, and there you are, clean. So, what's next?

You're going back to the same environment, the same world that put you in harm's way in the first place. It's like going back to square one; every addict knows that. The million-dollar question is: how are you going to avoid that?

There is no easy answer, but first and most important, you've got to change your lifestyle.

What is a lifestyle, you might ask? Well, lifestyle is the way you used to live, how you used to do things. Lifestyle is your hobbies, your habits, your friends, your daily activities, your routines, and your way of thinking.

You might be thinking, "I'm not going to change my lifestyle just to stay clean. That is almost impossible."

I say, that is a myth. It is actually not that hard at all. Start small and simple.

Again, remember every journey in life starts with one little step.

Here are the Seven Golden Columns of Lifestyle:

1. Habits:

"Only the wisest and the stupidest of men never change"
—Confucius

Change your old bad habits. For example, if you used to go to bars, to nightclubs, or to parties and you used to drink or use drugs there, well, you need to stop that immediately. Today, not tomorrow. If you used to travel all the time just to experience new foods and drinks or join parties, well, it is time to stop that, too. If you used to have a habit of coming home from work and sitting on the couch watching TV and eating and drinking alcohol, you need to stop doing that. If you used to call so-and-so to hang out every evening, well, that needs to go. If you like to watch a game or a show on TV while drinking beer or having a glass of wine, you need to stop it.

If you think that you need Oxycodone or some other kind of painkiller because you have some vague pain and your doctor is prescribing it to you because you've been lying about the severity of it, then you either tell your doctor to stop it or change your doctor. In fact, you need to tell your doctor that you have a problem with addiction.

Even if you don't think you have a problem, you still need to live your life free of the control of bad habits, whether it's a drug or a condition. If you used to binge and purge so you could stay slim, you need to stop that cycle, because purging is not going to keep you slim. It will only keep you looking sick, feeling sick, and eventually getting sick.

People are creatures of habit, so unless you break your vicious cycle, you will relapse and return to your misery.

2. Music:

"Music is a moral law. It gives soul to the universe, wings to the mind, flight to the imagination, and charm and gaiety to life and to everything." —Plato (424–338 BC)

I can't emphasize enough the importance of learning or even perfecting a musical instrument. Learning an instrument—such as piano, guitar, violin, drums, or what have you—will keep you sharp, entertained, and occupied, and it will also give you a sense of joy and achievement in life like you've never experienced before. It will discipline you, and as you know, discipline is the second step of recovery. If you already know how to play an instrument, then you really need to perfect it and practice it on a daily basis. Make it a habit, a part of your routine; you don't just do it when you feel like it. It doesn't work that way. Remember, every little thing helps to keep you occupied and happy, and what is better than music?

Let's say your condition is alcoholism or drug addiction, for example, or perhaps being overweight or even having an eating disorder. This is going to help you to overcome those conditions. Music is food for the soul. Learning an instrument is more important than just listening to music, because you need to be proactive and not passive. You need to *make* music; you need to sharpen your senses and take a new challenge in your life. So if you think learning an instrument is optional, you are wrong; this is a very important column in recovery and you must take it seriously.

3. Pets:

"If there are no dogs in heaven, then when I die, I want to go where they went." —Unknown

Adopt a pet, like a cat, a dog, or even a bird, if you don't have one; this will keep you humbled and occupied. The animal will teach you a couple of things about life, such as unconditional love, loyalty, and simplicity. Having a pet in your life will also teach you responsibility and humility. You will receive so much love in return, love that you really need. You will appreciate life. Also, you will save an animal, and that is priceless.

Current medical research indicates that having a pet in your household will increase your life expectancy substantially. So having a pet in your life is not just a good idea, it is a great investment in your path to righteousness.

4. Friends & Partners:

"Never contract friendship with someone that is not better than thyself." —Confucius

Unless your friends are good friends with no drug problems or other conditions similar to the one with which you suffer, then you must find yourself some new friends. But don't go out of your way looking for them everywhere. Don't worry, it is only a matter of time until you find yourself hanging out with a new community. Remember the famous saying, "Birds of a feather flock together." This means they will find you, like it or not.

No more calling your smoking or drinking buddies, or those folks who you had something in common with when you had the condition. It is only a matter of time until they influence you and throw you down the drain again, and no matter how strong your will or your character is, they will get you. Say goodbye to those old buddies, and never feel bad about it, because you are actually doing yourself and them a favor.

What about your partner, your husband, or your wife? What if you believe they have a problem with a condition, and they are not getting help? Well, this rule applies to them also. Does that mean you need to get a divorce? Or leave the house? Well, you need to do the right thing for you and for your partner, meaning you need to enforce this rule in your life, and so politely you must discuss the situation with him or her.

You need to tell your partner that he or she must get help immediately, not next week or next month. If your partner does not share your views or does not think they have a condition, then you need to leave. You must get out of there, this way you are not only helping yourself, but helping them too. Because they need a wake-up call in their life, too. Don't feel bad about it; feel good about it, because you are doing them a huge favor, and one day they will greatly appreciate it.

5. **Exercise:**

"No citizen has the right to be amateur in the matter of physical training... what a disgrace it is for a man to grow old without even seeing the beauty and strength of which his body is capable."
—Socrates

If you had some sport as a hobby but you neglected it, then you need to pick it up again, and if you never had one, then pick up a new sport such as dancing, hiking, biking, golf, soccer, baseball, boxing, karate, Pilates, yoga, Zumba, etc. Alternatively, start going to the gym, and make it a habit. These are the doctor's orders, no matter how much you hate to work out. Remember, you need to make it a habit; no thinking or analyzing, because, like we said, "if you analyze it you paralyze it." So just do it.

Why am I making a big deal out of exercise? Because the benefits of exercise are endless. First of all, 10 minutes of exercise a day are equal to 10 mg of Prozac; 20 minutes are equal to 20 mg, but without the side effects. Prozac is an anti-depression and anti-anxiety medication that has a long list of side effects.

Exercise will get you in shape and make you look and feel younger; it will help you stay away from drugs because it will give you a natural high. Exercise increases the production of endorphins and other important neurotransmitters in your body, which are very important in keeping you happy and free of pain. Exercise will also steer you away from taking drugs because it will help you make better decisions in life. When you go the gym or enroll in a sport, you will meet people who usually do not use drugs, people who probably have a healthier lifestyle than those who do not exercise.

Remember, we are not judging people here, but you need every little bit of help you can get in your life to change your lifestyle, to stay clean and sober, and to conquer that condition you're suffering from. But what about those with anorexia nervosa, for example, who use exercise as a purging mechanism, to lose more weight, even though they are underweight already? Well, the answer is, persons with anorexia nervosa should not exercise more than 15 minutes a day, and people who are overweight must not work out more than an hour a day. Too much of anything is not a good thing.

6. **Reading:**

"You can't open a book without learning something." — Confucius

Read a book every night before you go to bed. It doesn't matter what kind of book, as long as you read. Of course, I would advise you to read something positive or humorous, or perhaps a self-help book. You don't have to read something about your condition; in fact, it is better not to. Read something different, something fun and entertaining.

You don't have to finish the entire book in one session, but it is important for you to let your imagination run wild, so to speak. Let your mind take you to places you've never been, places where you don't think about drugs, food, or any negative issues in your life. The book will train you and entertain you. You must exercise your brain, not just your body.

Reading will make you smarter and wiser in life; you will learn things you never knew before. In fact, reading might just open up another avenue in your life.

7. Food:

"Worthless people live to eat and drink, people of worth eat and drink to live." —Socrates (469–399 BC)

You're not going to eat just anything from now on. Food is never the object of affection. Food was not created for enjoyment; food exists in this world for you to survive, nothing more, nothing less. It is there to keep your body healthy and surviving. From now on, you must change the way you think about food, otherwise you will fall into the mode of food addiction and food obsession, which is the whole mark of obesity.

Of course, it is always good to eat something fresh and healthy and perhaps presentable, but getting obsessed with meals and food networks on TV or food shows is a pretty bad idea. Everything in life should be in moderation, including food. From now on, you're going to start eating healthy and in moderation.

From now on, you will start cooking or preparing simple meals: breakfast, lunch, and dinner, if possible (or at least cook your dinner). Don't let someone else cook it for you, because if you do, you will defeat the purpose. You don't know how to cook? That's even better, because from now on, you're going to learn how to cook. But remember, nowadays you don't even need to cook, because most things are sold cooked already and all you have to do is add something to it—a little salad, some spices, some dressings—and you're good to go.

Carbohydrates is your enemy and they cause weight gain. Humans are not designed to eat carbs as simple as that just like the fact that we are not designed to use drugs. Focus on vegetables, nuts, and seafood rather than meat. Read a simple cooking book—there are thousands of them all over bookstores. You can even download a recipe application on your mobile phone for free, and most recipes are actually free on the Internet, so you don't have any excuses. Be the master chef in your own kitchen, and stop watching cooking shows on TV. This way you're not only going to eat healthy and feel good about yourself, but also save your health and your money, and of course you'll be changing your lifestyle.

Now, you might ask, what does this have to do with my sobriety, with my condition? Well, everything or maybe nothing. Changing your food routine is a significant part of changing your lifestyle, changing old habits, keeping you healthy, keeping you occupied and entertained, helping you grow, saving you money, having something good to do in your life, making your spouse, your boyfriend, or your girlfriend happy, and the list goes on and on. It's all about discipline, and food is no different.

"A lion chased me up a tree, and I greatly enjoyed the view from the top." –Confucius.

In memory of my father, Soulaiman Laty (1929-1992), healer, philosopher, and a righteous man.

References:

The Analects by Confucius

The Book of the Dead by Ogden Goelet

Conversations of Socrates

Complete Works of Aristotle

The Bible

The Complete Works of Lao Tzu

The Tao Te Ching by Lao Tzu

The Art of War by Sun Tzu

The Book of Five Rings (The way of the Warrior) by Miyamoto Musashi

Twelve Steps and Twelve Traditions

Printed in Great Britain
by Amazon